A BUSINESS APPROACH TO LETTUCE FARMING

Complete Entrepreneurial Step By Step Guide To Lettuce Garden From Scratch

ZHURI HART

DISCLAIMER

This book is intended to provide general information and insights on adopting a business approach to farming. The content within is based on the author's knowledge and experiences up to the date of publication. It is essential to recognize that the field of agriculture is dynamic, influenced by various factors such as market conditions, climate, and regulatory changes.

Readers are advised to conduct thorough research, seek professional advice, and consider their unique circumstances before implementing any strategies or practices discussed in this book. The author and publisher disclaim any responsibility for the accuracy, completeness, or suitability of the information provided. The book is not a substitute for professional advice, and the author and publisher shall not be liable for any damages or losses arising from the use or reliance on the information presented herein.

Individual results may vary, and success in farming enterprises is contingent upon numerous variables. The author encourages readers to consult with relevant experts, agricultural extension services, and legal or financial professionals to tailor strategies to their specific needs and local conditions.

This book is not intended to be a comprehensive guide to all aspects of farming, and readers should exercise their judgment and discretion in applying the principles discussed. The author and publisher do not endorse any specific products, services, or companies mentioned in this book unless explicitly stated.

By reading this book, the reader acknowledges and accepts the inherent uncertainties in agricultural endeavors and agrees to use the information at their own risk.

TABLE OF CONTENTS

ABOUT THE BOOK

This book, "A Business Approach to Lettuce Farming," is a thorough manual designed to give lettuce growers the skills and know-how they need to be successful in the agricultural sector. The book gives a history and outline of lettuce growing in the introduction, highlighting its importance in the larger agricultural scene. This lays the groundwork for comprehending the goals of the book, which center on providing farmers with useful knowledge to cultivate lettuce successfully.

The book's examination of lettuce types is one of its main topics. This covers common varieties of lettuce in detail, offers advice on the varietal selection that is specific to the success of businesses and examines the several elements that affect the choice of lettuce varietal. By reading this section, farmers can be sure they are knowledgeable when making important choices about the kinds of lettuce to plant.

The book then discusses important aspects of growing lettuce, like choosing and readying a place. Insights into soil requirements and environment are provided to readers, along with advice on selecting the best site and using efficient soil preparation methods. There is also a lot of discussion on planning and designing the lettuce farm, including infrastructure, irrigation systems, farm layout, and greenhouse farming factors.

A large chunk of the book is devoted to best practices in lettuce cultivation, including crop care, pest and disease control, transplanting procedures, nursery management, and seed sowing. The emphasis on ideal growing conditions—such as the right amount of light and temperature, managing nutrients, and crop rotation techniques—guarantees that growers will be able to establish an atmosphere that supports healthy lettuce growth.

To retain quality, the book goes beyond harvesting and post-harvest handling, offering insights on assessing harvest readiness, harvesting methods, and post-harvest handling procedures. An in-depth discussion is given to marketing tactics for growers of lettuce, such as identifying consumer demand, fostering connections with distributors, and creating eye-catching packaging and branding.

A full analysis of financial management and planning for lettuce farming concludes this extensive guide. This covers financial risk management, profitability evaluation, cost analysis, and budgeting. With all of these elements together, "A Business Approach to Lettuce Farming" becomes a valuable tool for lettuce growers, providing a comprehensive view of the crop from planning to profitability.

CHAPTER ONE

LETTUCE FARMING INTRODUCTION

THE HISTORY AND SYNOPSIS OF LETTUCE PRODUCTION

With its roots in agricultural customs, lettuce growing has become an essential part of the world's food production system. Asteraceae is a family of leafy green vegetables that is widely farmed for its nutritious value, various variations, and soft leaves. Lettuce farming has a long history and was used extensively in both culinary and medicinal uses in ancient cultures.

To meet the rising need for this adaptable leafy green, lettuce farming has evolved into a complex sector that embraces contemporary technologies and sustainable methods.

The rise of lettuce growing as a major contribution to both local and worldwide markets has been seen by the agriculture industry. The appeal of lettuce is due to its mild flavor and crisp texture, as well as its versatility in a variety of culinary uses. Lettuce is a basic item that may be used in a variety of recipes, including salads, sandwiches, and wraps.

It also adds flavor and nutrition. It is essential to comprehend the history and overview of lettuce farming to fully appreciate the complex procedures that go into growing, harvesting, and distributing the crop.

LETTUCE'S SIGNIFICANCE IN THE AGRICULTURAL SECTOR

Beyond its use as food, lettuce plays a significant role in the agriculture sector. Because it creates jobs and sustains livelihoods, lettuce farming helps keep many places economically stable. Lettuce is a major contributor to the promotion of a balanced and nutrient-dense diet because of its cultivation, which coincides with the growing global emphasis on good eating practices.

Furthermore, organic farming methods, water conservation, and environmentally friendly techniques have become more important in lettuce farming practices as they adjust to contemporary sustainability norms.

The fact that lettuce is resilient and adaptable to a wide range of growth environments highlights its importance in the agricultural industry. Its ability to adapt has made it easier to grow in many parts of the world, which has increased its availability and accessibility to consumers. Due to its low calorie and high nutritional content, lettuce has come to represent healthy eating, which has increased demand for the produce and guaranteed a constant crop for lettuce growers.

Learning about the history and scope of lettuce farming reveals a vibrant sector that has developed into a vital part of the contemporary agricultural economy.

CHAPTER TWO

KNOWING THE DIFFERENT TYPES OF LETTUCE

COMMON LETTUCE TYPES

A versatile and popular leafy green vegetable, lettuce is available in a variety of forms, each with unique qualities, tastes, and textures. Loose-leaf, Butterhead, Romaine, and Iceberg lettuces are some of the most popular varieties.

Because of its mild flavor and crisp texture, iceberg lettuce is a popular option for salads and sandwiches. But romaine lettuce, which is frequently used in Caesar salads, has longer leaves and a stronger flavor. Butterhead lettuce has a mild, buttery flavor and loose heads with soft leaves.

As the name suggests, loose-leaf lettuce has a loose head and is valued for its easy picking of individual leaves, which adds variation to salads.

SELECTING VARIABLES FOR BUSINESS SUCCESS

For any commercial endeavor in the agriculture or food industry to be successful, selecting the appropriate types of lettuce is essential. Consumer tastes, regional climate, and market demand are all carefully taken into account during the selection process. Given its broad appeal, iceberg lettuce could be a wise option for manufacturing and distribution in large quantities, serving a variety of consumer needs.

Having a competitive advantage, however, can come from knowing the local market and its preference for particular lettuce varieties, such as Romaine or specialist kinds. Additionally, for long-term commercial success, varietal selection is heavily influenced by elements including yield, disease resistance, and shelf life. Growing lettuce varieties that suit changing customer preferences can be facilitated by working with regional markets and chefs to stay up to date on new trends.

ELEMENTS AFFECTING LETTUCE VARIETAL SELECTION

The selection of lettuce cultivars is influenced by several factors, including market demands, farming techniques, and environmental factors. Climate is a major factor since different types of lettuce require different amounts of moisture and temperature to flourish. Choosing types that are appropriate for the area is made easier by having a thorough understanding of the local climate and soil composition. Varietal selection is guided by market demand, which includes both consumer preferences and commercial viability.

For example, picking lettuce kinds that fits with heirloom or organic food trends can increase marketability if these product preferences are on the rise. Another important consideration is disease resistance, which has a big impact on crop quality and output. Farmers frequently take into account how well a lettuce variety will generally adapt to their farming techniques, such as irrigation techniques and pest control tactics.

A thorough grasp of consumer trends, local circumstances, and agricultural dynamics is necessary to successfully navigate the wide range of lettuce cultivars. Common varieties of lettuce, including Butterhead, Romaine, Iceberg, and Loose-leaf, each have certain qualities to offer. However, a careful varietal selection process that takes into account elements like market demand, climate adaptability, and disease resistance is necessary for effective growing for commercial purposes. Growers can increase their chances of success in the cutthroat world of agriculture and food production by matching lettuce types with these factors.

CHAPTER THREE

CHOOSING AND SETTING UP THE SITE

CONDITIONS OF THE SOIL AND CLIMATE

The temperature and soil characteristics of the chosen area have a critical role in the success of lettuce cultivation. As a cool-season crop, lettuce is sensitive to intense heat and grows best in moderate temperatures. Generally speaking, the ideal temperature range for growing lettuce is between 60°F and 70°F (15°C and 21°C). It is imperative to evaluate the potential site's climate to make sure it fits these requirements. Lettuce also prefers soils that drain well and have a high water-holding capacity. Loamy or sandy loam soils are often selected because they hold enough moisture to support crops while offering appropriate drainage and aeration.

SELECTING THE IDEAL SITE FOR LETTUCE FARMING

The process of deciding where to grow lettuce requires a thorough examination of many different aspects. Exposure to sunshine is crucial since lettuce needs a lot of light to grow to its full potential. It is crucial to choose a location that receives full sun exposure to encourage healthy leaf development and avoid problems like bolting or elongation. Additionally, closeness to water sources is an important factor in enabling effective irrigation and maintaining stable soil moisture levels. It's also critical to analyze the microclimates in the selected area because elements like wind exposure and frost susceptibility can have a big impact on growing lettuce. The overall performance of the lettuce farm is influenced by the selection of a location shielded from severe winds and pockets of frost.

METHODS FOR PREPARING SOIL

A key component of growing lettuce is preparing the soil well, which affects the crop's growth and output. Soil testing to determine the composition and nutrient levels of the soil is the first stage in soil preparation. Adjustments can be made in light of the findings to make up for deficits and establish the best conditions for growth. Compost or well-rotted manure are examples of organic matter that can be added to improve soil fertility, structure, and water retention. To break up compacted layers and generate a loose, aerated soil profile, vigorous soil plowing is necessary. You can use raised beds to stop water logging and enhance drainage. Furthermore, adding a balanced fertilizer before to planting supplies the nutrients required for wholesome lettuce growth.

Careful assessment of the climate and soil conditions, deliberate site selection, and rigorous soil preparation methods are critical to the success of lettuce cultivation. Farmers may establish an atmosphere that best supports the growth and development of lettuce by coordinating these variables, which will ultimately guarantee a plentiful crop.

CHAPTER FOUR

ORGANIZING AND CREATING A LETTUCE FARM

INFRASTRUCTURE AND FARM LAYOUT

The infrastructure and architecture of your lettuce farm are crucial to achieving maximum productivity and efficiency while planning and designing it. The design must be carefully considered to meet the unique requirements of growing lettuce. Take into account elements including accessibility, wind patterns, and sunshine exposure. Since lettuce prefers bright light, it is best to plan the fields to receive as much sunlight as possible.

Planning for infrastructure entails creating the facilities that are necessary to run the farm efficiently. This contains special locations for growing, gathering, and preparing lettuce. Make sure that routes are arranged in a way that makes it simple for people and equipment to move about.

Convenient locations are needed for seed, fertilizer, and harvested crop storage facilities. Sustainable farming can also be aided by integrating eco-friendly techniques into the infrastructure design.

LETTUCE IRRIGATION SYSTEMS

Given the high water requirement of lettuce production, efficient irrigation is essential. Because drip irrigation systems are so effective at getting water straight to the root zone, they are frequently used in lettuce production. By using this technique, the risk of diseases linked to overhead watering is decreased and water waste is minimized. Consider elements like soil type, water quality, and the particular water requirements of lettuce at various growth stages while planning the irrigation system.

Irrigation system automation can improve accuracy and productivity. By using sensors to track soil moisture content, water distribution can be automatically adjusted; guaranteeing lettuce plants get the right quantity of moisture. Furthermore, a well-thought-out drainage system must be included to avoid water logging, which can harm lettuce plants.

CONSIDERING THE GREENHOUSE EFFECT

To grow lettuce, greenhouses provide a controlled environment that enables growers to prolong the growing season and shield crops from unfavorable weather. Think about things like orientation, ventilation, and temperature control while designing your greenhouse.

A properly oriented building maximizes its exposure to sunshine, while efficient ventilation keeps heat and humidity from building up and lowers the risk of illness.

Maintaining the ideal growth environment requires temperature control methods like heating and cooling systems. You can use shade netting or drapes to control light levels and shield lettuce plants from direct sunshine.

In addition, greenhouse constructions need to be built to resist environmental stresses like high winds and persistent snowfall.

Careful planning and design play a major role in a lettuce farm's success. The design and infrastructure need to be as efficient as possible, and irrigation and greenhouse concerns need to be in line with the particular needs of lettuce growing. You may optimize your total yield and cultivate lettuce in a healthy environment by implementing these ideas into your farm design.

CHAPTER FIVE

BEST METHODS FOR GROWING LETTUCE

MANAGEMENT OF NURSERIES AND SEED SOWING

The key to growing lettuce well is managing the nursery and planting the seeds correctly. To guarantee consistent germination and healthy seedlings, premium seeds from reliable vendors are required.

It's important to select the correct seedling tray or container to allow enough room for the growth of roots. For seedling growth, the nursery environment should be kept at the ideal humidity, temperature, and light levels.

Promoting healthy seedling development requires careful consideration of the substrate composition, spacing, and depth of seed sowing.

Maintaining a balance between retaining moisture and avoiding soggy conditions requires adequate watering.

It's critical to regularly check seedlings for pests and illnesses during the nursery stage to stop problems from spreading to the field.

TECHNIQUES FOR TRANSPLANTATION

Careful planting methods help ensure the crop's success throughout this crucial stage of the lettuce-growing process. When seedlings reach the proper developmental stage—usually when they have enough roots and true leaves—they should be transplanted. Plants should be spaced appropriately to provide the best possible light penetration and airflow, which lowers the danger of illness.

Handling seedlings carefully during transplanting is essential to prevent harm to the roots and foliage. Watering as soon as possible after transplanting aids in soil settling and lessens transplant shock.

Mulching the area surrounding the transplants helps keep the moisture in and keeps weeds out.

Transplanting at a lower temperature during the day can also help the seedlings experience less stress.

CROP UPKEEP AND CARE

Lettuce needs constant attention and upkeep during its growing season. To keep leaves from becoming stressed or bitter, adequate irrigation is crucial, with an emphasis on maintaining constant moisture levels. Due consideration should be given to the precise nutrient needs of lettuce while fertilizing. Timely modifications to watering, fertilization, and other cultural activities are made possible by routinely monitoring the health and growth of plants.

To avoid competing for nutrients and lower the chance of disease transmission, weed control is essential. Pruning damaged or overgrown leaves regularly promotes a healthier, more compact plant.

To reduce the risk of pests and soil-borne illnesses, crop rotation is advised. In addition, giving lettuce plants some shade during periods of strong sunlight helps shield them from heat stress.

MANAGEMENT OF PESTS AND DISEASES

Successful lettuce cultivation requires careful control of pests and diseases. It is imperative to do routine pest scouting to identify early infestations, including aphids, caterpillars, and snails. Integrated pest management (IPM) tactics can include encouraging natural predators and beneficial insects.

Maintaining adequate hygiene, including sanitizing tools and equipment, is essential to preventing disease. Crop rotation aids in disrupting soil-borne pathogens' life cycle. Considering their effects on beneficial species and possible residues on harvested produce, fungicides and insecticides should be used sparingly. The best way to stop illnesses from spreading throughout the crop is to identify them early and take appropriate action, including eliminating contaminated plants.

Good lettuce growing depends on using best practices in crop care, pest and disease management, transplanting, and seed sowing.

CHAPTER SIX

IDEAL CONDITIONS FOR GROWTH

TEMPERATURE AND LIGHT NEEDS

Temperature and light needs have a major impact on the ideal growing conditions for plants. The success of plant growth and development is largely dependent on these two variables. Certain temperature ranges are ideal for the growth of particular plants. For example, lettuce needs to be kept at a cool, comfortable temperature—60 to 70 degrees Fahrenheit, or 15 to 21 degrees Celsius. Too hot or too cold of a temperature can impede germination, stunt plant growth, and eventually lower output.

Another important element affecting plant growth is light. Through the process of photosynthesis, plants use light energy to transform sunlight into vital nutrients. As a cool-season crop, lettuce typically needs 12 to 16 hours of light every day to thrive to its full potential.

The overall quality of the lettuce might be impacted by extended and weak stems caused by inadequate light exposure. Particularly in areas with little sunlight, growers frequently use supplemental lighting systems, such as LED or fluorescent lights, to make sure the plants get the light they need.

HANDLING NUTRIENTS IN LETTUCE

For lettuce production to promote healthy plant growth and high-quality yields, effective nutrition control is essential. At various phases of its growth cycle, lettuce has distinct nutritional needs that need to be satisfied. Potassium, phosphorus, and nitrogen are the main macronutrients that are needed in different amounts. Potassium promotes general plant health and disease resistance, phosphorus aids in root formation, and nitrogen is essential for the growth of leafy greens.

Lettuce also needs micronutrients such as zinc, iron, and manganese in addition to macronutrients. These components are crucial for the activation of enzymes and other metabolic activities in plants. To give the proper nutrients in the right amounts, a balanced fertilization regimen using organic or synthetic sources must be implemented. To determine nutrient levels and help growers modify their fertilization techniques, soil testing is frequently used.

CROP ROTATION TECHNIQUES

A sustainable farming technique called crop rotation is gradually switching up the kinds of crops planted in a given region from one season to the next. This tactic aids in disrupting the cycles of disease and pests, enhancing soil fertility, and maximizing nutrient usage. The implementation of efficient crop rotation strategies is crucial in the growth of lettuce as it aids in the prevention of soil-borne illnesses and pests that may negatively impact the plants.

Crops from several botanical families should be alternated in a lettuce crop rotation strategy. This aids in sabotaging the life cycles of certain pests and diseases that could harm lettuce. Because legumes can fix nitrogen in the soil for the benefit of future crops like lettuce, legumes like peas and beans are frequently used in crop rotation schemes. Furthermore, adding cover crops while the land is fallow enhances the fertility and structure of the soil.

Careful fertilizer management, thoughtful crop rotation, and a thorough grasp of temperature and light requirements are all necessary to produce the best growth conditions for lettuce. Growers may contribute to effective and sustainable agricultural practices by improving the general health and production of lettuce crops by addressing these fundamental ideas.

CHAPTER SEVEN

HARVESTING AND HANDLING AFTER HARVEST

HOW TO ASSESS HARVEST PREPAREDNESS

Calculating Harvest A key component of effective crop management is readiness, which entails a thorough evaluation of numerous variables to guarantee the best possible yield and quality. The taste, texture, and nutritional value of crops are all strongly impacted by the time of harvest.

A crop's readiness for harvesting is mostly dependent on its size, color, hardness, and level of maturity, among other characteristics. Furthermore, certain crops can need special markers, such as the sugar level in fruits or the grain's seed maturity. Farmers may make educated decisions about when to harvest, balancing output maximization with the assurance of exceptional quality, by routinely monitoring and observing these parameters.

TECHNIQUES FOR HARVESTING

Harvesting techniques are a broad category that includes a variety of approaches designed to address the unique needs of various crops. Harvesting by hand entails selecting fruits, vegetables, or flowers by hand; this technique is frequently applied to fragile or valuable crops. On the other side, mechanized harvesting uses equipment such as combine harvesters to harvest grains on a big scale, increasing productivity and lowering labor costs. Harvesting with precision is crucial to minimizing crop damage and maximizing production overall. The kind of crop, the production volume, and the surrounding environment all play a role in choosing the best harvesting method. Harvesting techniques must be implemented successfully using a blend of technology, experience, and best practices.

HANDLING AFTER HARVEST TO PRESERVE QUALITY

The quality and shelf life of harvested crops are greatly enhanced by post-harvest handling. After harvest, handling needs to be done immediately and properly to avoid physical damage, minimize moisture loss, and limit exposure to pathogens.

Preserving nutritional value, avoiding degradation, and preserving freshness are the key goals of post-harvest treatment. To accomplish these objectives, procedures like cooling, sorting, and cleaning are frequently used. By controlling humidity and temperature, cold storage facilities help perishable commodities keep their market life longer by delaying ripening.

Managing temperature, packing, and storage all work together to preserve quality throughout post-harvest processing.

For instance, to slow down respiration rates and postpone ripening, fruits and vegetables are frequently preserved in controlled environments. Care must be taken while selecting packaging materials and techniques to shield crops from illnesses, pests, and physical harm.

Furthermore, the application of quality control procedures, such as routine testing and inspections, guarantees that only superior produce is distributed to customers. In addition to increasing the market value of crops, effective post-harvest handling lowers food waste and satisfies consumer demands for fresh, wholesome goods.

CHAPTER EIGHT

MARKETING TECHNIQUES FOR PRODUCERS OF LETTUCE

COMPREHENDING THE DEMAND IN THE MARKET

A thorough grasp of consumer demand is essential for farmers to succeed in the cutthroat world of lettuce production. This entails carrying out in-depth market research to pinpoint consumer trends, preferences, and unique demands.

Farmers should examine variables including demand fluctuations throughout the year, geographical preferences, and consumer demographics.

Farmers of lettuce may ensure a consistent and timely supply that meets consumer demand by proactively planning their planting dates and remaining aware of market factors. This proactive strategy can improve profitability, cut waste, and maximize output.

DEVELOPING CONNECTIONS WITH PURCHASERS

For lettuce growers, building trusting relationships with purchasers is essential to a successful marketing plan. Building relationships with different supply chain participants, such as wholesalers, restaurateurs, and retailers, is part of this. It's crucial to establish consistency and quality in products when fostering trust and dependability. Understanding the needs and interests of customers requires effective communication. Open communication among farmers is essential for getting input, resolving issues, and adjusting to shifting market needs. Joint marketing campaigns and tailored product offerings are two examples of collaborative activities that can strengthen these bonds and create mutually profitable long-term collaborations.

PACKAGING AND BRANDING

In a crowded market, differentiating lettuce goods is mostly dependent on effective packaging and branding. It is recommended that farmers focus their time and resources on crafting aesthetically pleasing and enlightening packaging that accentuates the sustainability, quality, and freshness of their produce. Using ecologically friendly packaging materials could also be warmly received by customers who care about the environment.

Creating a unique brand identity aids in the market presence and brand recognition of lettuce growers. This comprises coming up with an eye-catching logo, selecting eye-catching brand colors, and developing an original brand story.

In addition to drawing in customers, a strong brand presence gives purchasers confidence, which boosts revenue and market share.

Lettuce growers can achieve success with their marketing efforts by developing a thorough grasp of consumer demand, cultivating a solid rapport with purchasers, and making strategic investments in branding and packaging.

Lettuce growers may get a competitive edge in the market and secure long-term success by matching their methods to consumer tastes, working with important stakeholders, and presenting their produce in an eye-catching and unique way.

CHAPTER NINE

PLANNING AND MANAGEMENT OF FINANCES

SETTING A BUDGET FOR LETTUCE FARMING

Successful budgeting is essential to the success of lettuce farming because it enables growers to plan and allocate resources effectively. Estimating costs and income related to growing lettuce entails budgeting and taking into account labor, irrigation, equipment, seeds, and fertilizers. Making a thorough budget that accounts for both variable and fixed expenses is crucial. While fixed expenses, like equipment upkeep, are largely constant, variable costs, like labor and seeds, can change depending on variables like market demand and weather.

To maintain resilience in the face of uncertainty, budgets for lettuce farming should also include backup plans for unforeseen circumstances like bad weather or pest infestations. Farmers may improve overall financial performance, maximize resource use, and make well-informed decisions by keeping an eye on and making adjustments to the budget throughout the farming cycle. Lettuce farmers can increase the probability of a profitable crop and manage their finances proactively by creating a well-organized budget.

PROFITABILITY AND COST ANALYSIS

To ascertain whether growing lettuce is profitable, a comprehensive cost study must be performed. This entails figuring out and classifying all of the expenses related to farming, from preparing the land to harvesting. It is necessary to take into account both direct costs, such as labor, seeds, and fertilizer, and indirect costs, including overhead and equipment depreciation. Farmers can comprehend the full financial consequences of their business through accurate cost allocation.

Examining the correlation between expenses and earnings is essential for determining profitability. To assess the total financial viability of their lettuce farming endeavor, farmers can compute important financial measures including gross profit margin, net profit margin, and return on investment.

Frequent cost analysis enables farmers to make well-informed decisions and find opportunities for cost savings or productivity gains. In the ever-changing agricultural context, resilience and sustainability are ensured by constant profitability assessment.

MANAGEMENT OF FINANCIAL RISK

Given the industry's vulnerability to several risks, financial risk management is essential to the success of lettuce farming. Unpredictable weather patterns, fluctuating input costs, and volatility market pricing are a few examples of the variables that can cause risks. Various risk management techniques can be used by farmers to lessen these difficulties and safeguard their financial interests.

In the business of growing lettuce, diversification is essential to financial risk management. Farmers can spread their risks and lessen reliance on a single source of income by growing many types of lettuce or taking part in complementary agricultural practices. Using financial tools like insurance policies can also act as a safety net against unanticipated occurrences like crop failure or natural catastrophes.

Proactive risk management requires constant observation of market trends and knowledge of outside influences on lettuce prices. To overcome any obstacles together, farmers need also build trusting bonds with financial institutions, distributors, and suppliers. Lettuce growers may guarantee their long-term viability and improve their financial stability by implementing effective risk mitigation strategies and strategic planning.

www.ingramcontent.com/pod-product-compliance
Lightning Source LLC
Chambersburg PA
CBHW070839290526
45795CB00002B/922